Voices

Voices

Poems Inspired by God

Karen J Chisholm

Copyright © 2017 Karen J Chisholm

Library of Congress Control Number:2017915293
ISBN: Hardcover   978-0-9994105-3-0
         Softcover   978-0-9994105-6-1
         eBook   978-0-9994105-9-2
         Audiobook   978-0-9994105-2-3

All rights reserved. No part of this book may be reproduced or transmitted in any form or by any means, electronic or mechanical, including photocopying, recording, or by any information storage and retrieval system, without permission in writing from the copyright owner.

All images were created for and are the property of Karen J Chisholm.

All scripture quotations, unless otherwise indicated, are taken from the King James Version of the Bible.

This book was printed in the United States of America.

First Edition

To order additional copies of this book, contact:

Without Price Publishing
P.O. Box 57133
Webster, TX 77598
(281) 899-8789

email: withoutpricemp@gmail.com
     or visit
www.karenjchisholm.com

Other books by Karen J Chisholm:

I AM with You: Poems Inspired by God
Tough as Nails: Poems Inspired by God

This book is dedicated to the Glory of God

With special thanks to:

My family:
My dad, Alva M. Patterson
My mom, Genevieve (Pat) Patterson
My brother, Duane Patterson
My sister, Lynette Neubauer

You take me as I am and love me anyway.
This is the way God loves us all,
and I learned it first with you.
I love you too.

and

Those whose voices God shared with me.
He heard your prayers.
He always will.
He answers.

Table of Contents

I HEAR YOU
- Voices 1

COME TO ME
- The Busy Mom 9
- To the Busy Mom 11
- So Much to Do 13
- Outdoing 15
- Busy 18
- Rest 21
- Humble 24

APPLYING THE OIL OF JOY
- Not Even Death 29
- Know Why 31
- Heaven 33
- God, Where Were You? 34

LIFTED IN MY ARMS
- Helpless 39
- Remember to Be Thankful 42
- Down 44
- No Answer 47
- Look Up 50
- Hello, Jesus 52
- How Long, O Lord? 56
- The Same 58

SET FREE INDEED
- Alone 63
- Feelings 66
- So Alone 68
- Never Alone 70
- Dying Moments 73
- The Past 76
- Close 79
- Difficult Times 81
- Come 84
- No Matter 87
- The Last Prisoner 89
- Love My Neighbor, My Enemy 91
- Keep Walking 94

CHOSEN TO SERVE ME
- The Police Officer 99
- My Cop 102
- The Firefighter 104
- My Firemen 106
- The Soldier 108
- The Uniform 110
- My Servants 112

AUTHOR
- About the Author 117

Foreword

I AM.

Wherever you are, I AM.

I will open your understanding to focus on and comprehend the Love that I AM.

At present, you look at Me as Love, and yourself as Not Love. I AM changing your spiritual perception. Only know that in the beginning this will not feel right. Nevertheless, you must keep yourself open to change, open to Me, open to love yourself. This paves the way and opens you to Love.

Stay constantly aware of Me, always aware of My Presence. Open yourself to Holy Spirit. Do not use this time to judge and measure; use it to focus on and perceive Me in every situation. I will lead you into truth. Hold everything up to My Word. Let My Spirit reveal truth to you. Withhold judgment and, instead, receive truth.

I will sort it out for you. Trust Me.

Father

Prologue

Write for Me, Child.
This word will be the title of your next book: Voices.
Would you like to begin?

Oh, yes, Lord, keep on speaking!

Do not consider what it will be about. Simply trust and write. I will choose what I want published. I AM.

Beloved, you are Mine. All I AM is yours. I have said this to you before and you humbled yourself out of believing it. I want you to reconsider it today. Everything about Me is available to you and is available through you to others. Whosoever will. Are you a whosoever or are you the exception? When God offers His abundant ability as resource for you to draw on to minister life to those around you who are in need, and you think to do so is presumptuous, who gets glory?

No one. There is no glory.

And who wins?

The enemy.

EXACTLY.
So, the question today is, will you be My vessel, My tool, My conduit to release My abundant ability to others?

This is going to be published one day and so I now turn to the reader and I ask you:

Will you be My vessel? My tool? My conduit to release My abundant ability and resources to others?

I am not looking for "stars" or showoffs or even people who are comfortable making conversation with strangers. I AM calling everyday, unspecial people made special because they allow Me to use them on a daily basis as I see fit. They pray often, they come to find Me in My Word, they learn of Me and worship Me. I AM their only God. They know and are deeply convinced there is no other God. They follow Jesus, the Christ, the Messiah, Son of God and Son of man, and in His name, they pray. I fill them with My Presence and those who know Me recognize My Spirit in them. They *slosh* holiness onto people they meet without saying a word. There are people who don't want to be around them because of the discomfort that brings. There are the others who are angry with them and cannot get over it. All these things fall on Me. I AM. So, reader, will you serve Me?

So, Child, will you serve Me? Will you presume upon our relationship? Presume upon My love? Elijah presumed. Elisha presumed. I want you to presume too. Believe I AM fulfilling your words spoken over others in prayer. Will you speak the huge miracles I long to perform? Will you bring Me great glory? Will you trust Me to do what you cannot do? I AM looking for willing vessels who will not draw back when I bring attention, when I bring notoriety, when My presence in you brings opposition and danger and tears.

Will you be the one? May I spend your life for the kingdom? Will you be the tool in My hand? A pencil, a sword, a lifeline, a stumbling block, a joy, a blessing, a rock of offense? Will you be Jesus for Me? Will you allow Jesus in you to continue to minister to souls who want to be saved?

Answer slowly. Count the cost for both yes and no. Sleep on it. Take time to write out the what-ifs.

Child, when you made the decision to give your life to Me, you counted the cost. You wrote down a list of the worst things that could happen. You visualized each and compared it to new life in Jesus Christ, evaluating whether you could follow through on your commitment in each case.

The day you reached the end of the list:

Your marriage
Your home
Your children
Your job
Your reputation
Your provision

Your resolve was strong. You would keep your commitment. You would follow Christ. You have never wavered in your decision through grief and loss and overwhelming shame and guilt. You have never let go of My hand through sin and temptation and poverty and riches and blessings and hardship and depression and wellness. You are Mine.

Mine.

Mine alone.

And now, I am asking you to go for Me. Continue praying for those you meet, those who despitefully use you, those in authority over you, those who love you, and those who doubt you. Give them all to Me, and do whatever I tell you.

As you begin, I will guide, as I did the first book: *I AM with You*. That project spiraled completely out of your control and will continue to grow and spread until it fulfills My vision for it. My Spirit is going before it and hovering over it and accompanies it wherever it is sold or given away, or spoken of. I AM anointing anyone who uses that book as a teaching tool and My Presence is on every word spoken when it is read. It washes over the hearers and fills them with truth-telling understanding if they are Mine. Each one will want to share the book and it will be gifted to many continuously in the next year and beyond.

I AM with You, always with you
To the end of the age
And beyond . . . *Father*

I Hear You

Voices

God Speaking March 22, 2017

Voices, I hear them
Every one known
Watch over, near them
Loved as My own

Grace well extended
Angels assigned
These My creation
Born spiritually blind

Each, every being
All doing their best
Making decisions
Work and then rest

All I AM wooing
I'm drawing to Me
Every one choosing
To serve self or Me

Those who well know Me
Are ones born again
Receiving the Good News
Sent down to men

They hear the Gospel
The good news of Christ
Receive with thanksgiving
Then destined to rise

Others, rejecting,
Have chosen their path
These a percentage
I've done the math

Enemy lying
Is telling them wait
Did God really say?
Who's this Jesus, the Gate?

Oh, that's not important!
The lie, practiced ease
Entices the senses
Entrapping, lives seize

All the time, loving
I'm calling their names
Come unto Me
Because life's not a game

When many talk to Me
They're mad as hell
Say if I'm listening
They sure can't tell

Blame Me not preventing
Horror been through
If I'm God, where am I
I'm right here with you

Some come so willingly
Born again, made new
Others struggle fighting Me
Blaming Me too

Think they'll have to give up
Their freedom, their lives
To be some poor schmuck
Who serves fake God in skies

The wise ones come looking
To prove I'm not real
If they look deep, long enough
Their doubt turns to zeal

Those looking for find Me
They ask, I will answer
Their faith seed takes root
Part of harvest I've planned for

They find My Great Love
Has been there all along
Kept them from dying
Then gave them new song

Others refuse
They don't want to know Me
Some prosper who shouldn't
Buys them power: steal the free

One day they'll answer
For wrong they have done
Right now they're laughing
Before judgment comes

And all the while loving
I offer to any
Salvation at My cost
My blood has saved many

Whosoever will
All are free to choose
Those who ask forgiveness
None of them I lose

The door of life stands open
The Light of Grace doth shine
Come while it is day
The night comes you won't find

All the time I'm with you,
Every choice you make
I hear all your voices
Know death angel takes

No matter accusation
I could have kept from pain
You don't know I have carried you
Provided air and rain

Good things, many blessings
Undeserved and free
Because I AM that I AM
Overarching Love is Me

I hear your thoughts, see actions
Know every choice that's made
For I AM always with you
In grief, I'm closer laid

Don't think you're all alone here
I'm with you every mile
If you cry out to Jesus
I'll wipe your tears, bring smile

So bring Me all your suffering
I'm tender toward the shunned
Even when accusing Me
I'm loving through the Son

Some will hear Me; some will not
I hear every voice
Know the content of each heart
Know the thought, the choice

I know the defiant
The fearful
The dedicated
The careless
The assuming
The unaware
The incapable

These precious . . .
Wanted . . .
Loved . . .

Voices

Come to Me

The Busy Mom

Inspired by God December 21, 2016

I have so much to do!
My children need my time.
I still want perfection
For all that I call mine.

The house, the meals, the clothes,
Shoes, purses, diaper bags.
The chopping and the shopping,
Good meals, dressed nice, no rags.

I still have dreams awakened
And goals and wants and plans.
None of them forsaken
Squeezed in between demands.

I love my husband, love my kids;
I want the best for them.
And for myself and all I love
To know Jesus within.

It takes more than intention
To come to know God well.
Did quiet time I mention?
Focus Him Who dwells.

He gives the sun each morning,
The warm, the cold, the light
Come from His treasures like the snow
Seen next day pure and white.

In places where are palm tress
And breeze o'er blue lagoon,
Moms are busy working too;
Like me, will be home soon.

It's hard to balance and have "me time"
But it can be done.
Joyous laughter, teasing banter
Keep our family one

Because we're busy!

To the Busy Mom
God Speaking December 21, 2016

I see all you do each day:
Sleep given to be ready
For the next day's necessaries,
Keep your family steady.

I know plans you've set aside
Know you, dear, through and through.
You're trusting Me to bring to pass
The plans I have for you.

Enjoy this moment; it will pass.
Right now, you're making memories.
What's in your heart, the gifts I've given,
Are growing in your reveries.

Don't pine for that which could have been;
You're living with your choices.
Appreciate life you live now:
Fast, busy pace, loud voices.

The precious lives placed in your care
Are yours for this short span.
On days you wonder how you'll make it,
I will hold your hand.

Stop and breathe, and look to Me
When there's too much to do.
A soft touch and your full attention
Are gifts you give them too.

For that is what you need from Me,
From husband you adore.
Like you, your kids and husband too
Will always welcome more.

Now get you up and start again;
It's off to work you go.
Know I AM with you through this day.
I have your back, you know,

You precious, busy mom.

So Much to Do
God Speaking October 23, 2014

You have so many tasks assigned
Yet others still accrue.
"No pressure. Can you get this done?"
"Sure," you say, "will do."

Every day, all day long,
You work for others' gain.
Your plans, your dreams, are set aside,
Faint hopes on lists remain.

You have a calling, know My voice,
Caught glimpses what would be,
Struggle to make daily choice
To do what pleases Me.

Goal before you, take the steps
And pass the milestones low.
Relationships and unexpected
Side trips progress slow.

Even working on the things
That matter, patience try.
The more you do, the more it takes
And silent time goes by.

"So much to do; wish I were two,"
The thought runs through your mind.
Most things get handled, tasks get done,
But not right ones sometimes.

The calling that I've given you
Brings benefits unseen,
Unknown by most 'til time reveals
The treasures this life screens.

And yet your daily bread arrives.
Provided—every need.
While you keep focused, heed My call,
And water My Word's seed.

Keep on coming, doing all
I give you here to do.
Just know I'm with you, bear you up,
Assist your follow-through.

You give Me time in early hours,
You contemplate My Word
And I remind throughout the day
The truth that you have heard.

You know faith comes by hearing
The truth that Jesus said.
Share what you have learned, encouraged
To write words in head.

Today is all the time you have,
This day I've given you.
Prioritize, not compromise
'Cause there's so much to do

Through you.

Outdoing

God Speaking June 18, 2016

Child, come here to Me. Focus on Me.
Give Me your burdens. Here you are free.
Let go of all cares. Lay burdens down,
Release frustration. Lose every frown.
Here.

Focus your thoughts now. Give Me your mind.
I will unravel; I will unwind.
Everything blocking dissolves in My Light.
All the wrong offered I'll turn into right.
Soon.

You don't have strength now to carry this load.
Your steps have faltered on this steep road.
Others you've carried who easily walk.
Stop here with Me now; Let's sit and talk.
Quietly.

Who are you pleasing when you say, "I'll do it"?
And why do you need to get around to it?
Yes, you are able, but they're able too.
When they state their plans, you try to outdo.
First.

One of the reasons frustration runs high:
Your expectations, unstated, don't fly.
Others would help if you'd mention your need.
But manipulation is habit indeed.
Oh my.

Obviously, what needs work is you.
But you must know first what you want to do.
Set goals to conquer before you begin.
Take time to ponder. Look deep within.
You.

All of this busyness just makes more work.
You don't want to do it, so you read and shirk.
But that builds the mountain of things you put off,
Deeds you have promised are done at your cost.
Why?

When you don't have goals or when they're unclear,
You do the unnecessary. You walk in fear.
You won't please others, accomplish your word
Because you have promised, but then you deferred.
Again.

Stop helping others to prove yourself better.
Stop finding fault and acting go-getter.
It's only in your head where you'll find a fight.
Nobody cares if you're wrong or you're right.
But you.

When you set your house in order, you'll find
You can be thoughtful; your words will be kind.
Peace will surround you wherever you go.
No one will notice you could have helped, so . . .
Don't.

"They've expectations" you're thinking.
That's right.
But if you've made plans, and you tell them,
They might

Offer to help, but for sure they won't ask
You to assist them accomplish their task.
Duh.

So, get a life. Set some goals.
Talk about your plans
Instead of complaining
To get attention.
It works.

Busy

God Speaking November 9, 2015

All of the busyness,
All of the flair,
All work combined
Cannot compare.
Accomplishing much
And doing of deeds
Just fills your time,
Addressing your needs.

Yet when things are done,
You'll have more things
Waiting to take your attention,
Time wings.
It zooms past, evaporates,
Marches, or flies
But what's done for Christ
Are the things that I prize.

And you are My treasure,
The one that I love,
The one with home waiting
And family above.
When you take the time
From your busy life here
To pray for another,
To bring sad ones cheer,

To visit the prisoner,
To play with their kids,
To give to the homeless,

The sick, meals with lids,
To lift up the hurting,
Show Love to the lost,
To be hands and feet
For Me at your cost,

You are fulfilling
My purpose and plan
By being to others
God come down to man.
For all of the working
You do for yourself
Can only remain
Like a book on a shelf
Passed by unremembered,
Ignored, or thrown out.
One new generations
Don't know, care about.

And when time has passed,
You're a name on a stone.
Or ashes long scattered,
Dispersed, and windblown.
For if you're remembered,
I want it to be
They talk of how you
Were like Jesus, like Me.

Your hands were like Christ's,
Full of comfort and prayer,
Your feet carried gospel
To men everywhere.
So now when you're busy,
Make it about these:
The lost and the hurting;
Bring them here to Me.

And when you are looking
At your bottom line,
Consider what you have
Is really all Mine,
Including your life
And your breath and your clothes.
So how will you answer
What you've done with those?

Those what? Why, the minutes
I gave you to use.
How spent, what to show for:
The truth or a ruse?
But you cannot cover
Your motives with Me.
I know every heart thought;
Each action I see.

Remember today
As you use what I've given,
Each intent, each action
Is well known in heaven.
And when all your seconds
Are used up and past,
Only what's done here
For Christ's sake will last.

What are *you* busy doing?

Rest

God Speaking December 26, 2016

Let not your heart be troubled:
Ye believe in God, believe also in Me.
(John 14:1)

Child, when you do well, you are pleased.
You ate more protein this week
You kept the dishes done
You found a lot of bargains
You still have money at week's end
You took time to exercise
You worshipped on Sunday
You paid your tithe
And the laundry is all done.

Is a clean house like a clean soul?
Yes. And no.
Your hard work and shrewd shopping
Are very satisfying.
It was a good day.
And now you think of all that's left to do,
Remember all the "someday" things waiting,
And see your life reduced to repetition.
Satisfaction melts away
And you mentally gird yourself,
For tomorrow it will be there to do again.

There is a better way.

Come to Me all who are tired,
Who continually carry a heavy load.

I will give you rest.
Deep soul rest.
The world cannot offer you rest;
You must leave the world to find it.
But the world is always with you.
Come to Me.
Sit quietly and focus on Me.
Wait silently and remember Me.
Remember I AM that I AM.

Instead of rehearsing what you think
You know about Me,
Leaving all conscious thought aside,
Focus on Me and become still.
Wait in silence and open yourself to Me.
Allow Me to do whatever I will.
Have no expectation, seek no answers.
Leave off repentance, regret, self-pity.
Just BE.

In the quietness, the waiting,
The absence of self,
My Peace will become evident,
Surprising you, relaxing you, filling you:
Deep soul peace.
Be patient. Stay here in My Peace.
Focus on Me. Dwell in this gift of peace
Where I offer you Myself freely.
Soon you will notice you feel full.
Sit just a little longer;
Soak in this peace the world cannot give.
Now go into your day.

Prayer, Bible study, will be deeper,
More meaningful.
Work, chores, self-care, your job,

Your ministry to others,
And all the details of life
Will be more satisfying, more rewarding
Because you are full of Me,
Operating in My strength.

You find joy in your work,
Have what you need,
Make good decisions,
Even your memory is improved.

All this because you took time
To focus on Me, laying aside responsibilities
To empty yourself in My Presence.
This small investment of time
Pays BIG dividends
Both in the spirit and in the natural.

Come again anytime.
Now go out in My power and
Have a blessed day.

Humble

God Speaking January 9, 2015

Child, you say . . .

How may I serve you?
What do you need?
I want to help where there's lack,
Yes, indeed.
I'll be the one who helps
Carry your load,
Walks the mile with you
On life's dusty road.

Here is another
Who needs helping hand.
I'll come alongside
And grab hold and stand.
There are so many things
I see need done.
I see opportunities.
Am I the only one?

And I tell you . . .

Child, you are generous,
Willing to share.
Some folks don't notice
And others don't care.
Some are too busy,
Overwhelmed with their own.
Some see, but pass by
And hurry on home.

There are sweet blessings
The humble receive.
Servants to others
And willing to please
Are humble like Jesus,
Not noticed by most.
These are My treasures
World 'round, coast-to-coast.

Sometimes extend themselves
Too far and tire
But feel good inside,
Helping down to the wire.
I love My servants,
The meek, apron-clad
Who would give their last dime
Though 'twas all that they had.

It's hard to get lower
In life than the humble.
Many want blessing
But at serving they stumble.
The difference is found
Right down inside the heart.
Being sold out to God,
Giving self's where it starts.

He who has bet the farm
I'm Who I said I was
Gives himself totally.
It shows in what he says and does.
He'll do a favor
For a friend after work
Neglecting his own food and rest;
He won't shirk.

The humble don't brag
And prefer work unnoticed.
Their reward, job well done;
Is their only focus.
Eventually, it comes to light
And others know and share.
The humble smile, get back to work,
For their reward is there.

Giving without show
Is being humble.
Thought you should know.

Applying the Oil of Joy

Not Even Death

Inspired by God May 10, 2016

You are gone, my son.
I can't hold you in my arms,
Your breath there on my cheek.
I cannot look into your eyes
Or hold your little hand.
You are gone.
You are gone.

I see your toys,
I hold your blankie tight.
It comforts me;
I, too, hold it in the night.
And you're gone.
You're gone.

I want to come to you,
To be there where you are.
I reach out to touch you,
But you have gone too far.

I'm trapped here in this body
For the number of my days,
But I will see your face again
And you and I embrace
When I'm gone.
I'm gone.

I'm folding laundry now;
It's busy work for hands.
Your little sock falls through
Numb fingers and I stand.

I shout at God and scatter clothes,
Release my tears of rage
Because I know that life's unfair;
Death comes at any age.

I know you're loved and wanted
Where God's taken you, but I don't care.
You're gone and I am hurting here.
I am hurting here . . . .

Now calm, I sense the Lord is near,
His Peace surrounds and holds me tight.
He whispers soft here in the night
And I can hear, "Not even death,"
So close I think I feel His breath.

And I remember what I know:
Jesus loves me. Even so,
I'll cherish all the memories,
The pictures, and the time.
You were my gift from God above
I'm glad that you were mine.

So glad that you were mine.

Know Why

God Speaking December 10, 2016

I hear your tears
I know your thoughts
For your worst fears
Came real

I heard you rage
As answers sought
Too young an age
Life steal

You handled well
Short life he led
Now you're a soul
Bereaved

When anger passed
And you lay still
On Me hope cast
Believed

One day you'll see
This child you loved
Then you'll be free
Restored

You'll hold him close
And never part
I'll hold you both
I'm Lord

See with own eyes
Answers all plain
God, only wise
Was right

Tears wiped away
Faith has reward
Joyous new day
Know why

Heaven

Inspired by God June 30, 2017

I'm playing with the other kids in heaven,
We're waiting for the time when you come home.
I can't wait for us to be together
Here in the kingdom Jesus calls His own.

I never need a sweatshirt or a comb here;
This new life's so fun - it never ends!
When you get here, I will hug and kiss you;
You'll carry me around and talk to friends.

There are lots of kids here; you should *see* them!
And you can watch me jump; I just can't wait!
I'm gonna ask Him can we ride His horse there
To where we meet you just inside the gate.

There's lots of cool stuff here I want to show you,
I know you'll come when Father says it's time.
I'll be the one who's yelling when I see you:
Look guys! There's my dad! Mom's right behind!

I can't wait to see you!
But for now,
I'll be playing.

God, Where Were You?

God Speaking April 13, 2017

When nothing's going on,
When answers aren't perceived,
When there is nothing pressing,
That's when you still believe.

I AM with your footsteps,
I AM still your guide.
This day just lean into Me;
I AM where you hide.

When circumstance means suffering,
When answers can't be found,
When your world's cracked and falling,
No prayer, no praise, no sound.

I'm with you when you're shattered,
Your loss too deep to grieve.
I'm here when you want answers
That now you can't receive.

I'm close as breath within you,
I carry you today.
The darkness overwhelming,
Nothing makes it go away.

Not one thing can be changed now.
It's over, done, and past.
But this oppressive darkness
Of the soul just seems to last.

You cannot receive comfort,
The pain's too deep to name.
You cannot bear politeness,
There's nothing that remains.

The guilt keeps burning deeper
Though you're a victim too,
But you're still here and breathing,
Don't know if you'll pull through.

The service was so touching,
The words were kind and soft.
But you've now found your anger
At God and self and loss.

You know you'll meet in heaven.
Why couldn't it be you?
A precious little life gone.
Your words: God, where were *You*!?!

I AM there.

Lifted in My Arms

Helpless

Inspired by God December 19, 2016

Lord, here I am in the bed of sickness.
Frailty has come to the bones once were strong.
I'm at the mercy of those paid to labor,
But there are so many they labor among.

I think it's my right to see smiling faces
Of caregivers called to this grace.
They do for others like me what is needed.
People with smiles work all over this place.

Once in a while, there's a young one who labors
Resenting attention must give,
Wishing someone would attend them instead,
Needing the notice to live.

I bear in mind this one will grow wiser;
I call their name out in prayer.
This young attendant has needs beyond mine,
Needs to know Your loving care.

In the next bed, the next room, down the hall,
Other beds hold bodies broken:
Lives that need mending as well as their bones;
I lie here merely a token.

Lord, we are, some of us, old in our years,
Once were ones took care of others.
Here in this hospital, here in this wing,
Lie fathers, moms, sisters, and brothers.

This is the place called skilled nursing, oh yes!
From bags here on poles: pain relief.
In other rooms somewhere, loved ones are crying;
Comes down to the end, hence the grief.

Today in this bed I can wrestle with why;
I can wish I had made better choices.
Or I can consider my caregivers' needs,
Lift their names up in prayer, even voiceless.

Thank you for doctors and nurses You've called:
Long schooling and hours of missed sleep.
Leaving young families at home while they labor,
Commitment to calling they keep.

These unsung heroes in ambulance, ward,
Bloodmobile, lab, nursing home
Are Your hands of caring for people that hurt
In quiet rooms lying alone.

Did, when You called them, they think of hard work?
What spark did You place in each heart?
The grace that You gave them, compassion for all,
Came from You, else they'd surely not start.

The long hours of learning, the years to prepare,
The cost both in dollars and time,
The doing without, resist giving up,
Has it been worth it all, this hard climb?

And what of the ones
Who must change my used diaper?
Are they working here to pay bills?
What are their dreams? What are their goals?
What their reward for my spills?

I see I've a calling now late in my life;
You are asking I pray now for these:
Caregivers all, each helping heart.
Reward unseen servants here, please.

Only I know how Your love in a heart
Touched me with mercy last night.
These caring hands, called through Your plan
Bring healing to set my world right.

Surprise! When I focus on others, I find
The pain passes by with the days.
I get well sooner, easier, less time
When my focus on others' need stays.

Caring about caregivers: this is my duty.
May I be the one who acts sweet
To your healing servants
With problems at home
Who put in long days on their feet.

I see I'm not helpless, though can't do for myself.
I'm helping my helpers through prayer.
Remind me, O Lord, when I get to go home
All these angels you've placed in my care

When I thought . . . I was helpless.

Atta girl. Now go into your day with joy.
I AM with you.   *Jesus*

Remember to Be Thankful

God Speaking November 21, 2013

Remember to be thankful;
Consider giving praise,
In good and bad and wonderful,
On sad and joyous days.

It is my will in Christ for you
To give thanks as you pray,
Rejoicing always, evermore
In big and little ways.

Remember to be thankful.

Praise Me in the little things;
Habits form that way
That draw you closer to Me
When hard times seem to stay.

Rejoice in tribulation
Joy opens prison doors.
Draw water from salvation
When persecution soars.

Be thankful.

Remember those who suffer,
For all must suffer some.
When you've lost all, then let it go;
New chapter has begun.

Instead of looking back then,
And living in the past,
Look up and give Me thanks
For new blessings coming fast.

Opportunities to praise Me abound
Cleverly disguised as trouble.
Remember...
Remember to be thankful.

#

Inspired of God January 19, 2017

I cannot tell my story.
Too different, too personal.
This woman would write of me.
Poetry she says.
God, you do not deserve my rhyme.
You don't care about me.
I don't care about you.

She sang me a song.
It said you want me.
I didn't feel a thing.
I said I didn't feel a thing.

No.
I didn't.

But I feel.
O, I certainly feel.
What can this white woman know?
What can she know about a woman of color
On the streets 24/7?

She hands me some money,
Thinks she's done some great thing.
When the sun leaves the sky, they will come.
They'll take all I have,
Then search me for more.
Things get real bad with no sun.

She will go home
To her husband and kids.
Her car and refrigerator full of food.
She'll pray some dry prayer,
Pass the plate then for seconds,
And all of them say it was good.

I guess you must be with her
'Cause you sure as hell ain't with me.
Why do you hate me so much?
I live on the streets, I get what I can,
I don't need no God; that's a crutch.

She thinks God is real,
Says she writes for you too.
Well you can't have my story—it's bad.
I don't want no pity, no syrupy smile.
None of that can undo what I've had.

I'm beaten and robbed,
Then beaten some more.
I have been raped more than once;
You don't care.
I'm hungry, forsaken,
And she's making rhyme.
If there is a God, come; I dare!

I don't exist to *quote* "deity."
I'm just a human who breathes.
My world's real small,
'Bout 3 city blocks.
I scavenge what someone else leaves.

So, prove it, you God!
Show yourself; you're so brave.
Come, bring it on, kill me now.
'Cause it won't get better here on the streets
But I'm here every morning somehow.

Prove you exist!
Prove you're real!
'Cause I ain't believin'
No sir.

I'm down.
You know how to get down?
Come on then.

No Answer

Inspired by God January 11, 2016

Some fall through the cracks.

No. I'm not that sloppy.
If I can make the universe by just speaking
And then create the human body,
With my breath cause it to live,
If I can create by miracle every newborn child,
If I can hear the tiniest doubt in every language,
And have heaven waiting when believers die,
Why
Can't I
See you?

I know you, child. I'm *in* your pain.
So close beside, My tears are rain.
Inside your silence, you scream Why?!!!
Think I'm not able, then deeply sigh.

Do you know Job? An old, old story.
An old, *old* story.
He served Me well, has brought Me glory.
Like him, I ask you, Why do you doubt Me?

I offer no answer for Myself.

You judge the Judge? You think I'm blind?
Where were you when I made mankind?
You cry Unjust! Say I don't care.
Best question: Why?!! Say life's not fair.

No.
It's not.

I do not answer.
No answer is due to any man or woman too.
For I AM God; My name I AM
And you were formed by My own hand.

Consider now, you're not alone.
I hear each prayer, know what you've done,
Know where you'll be a year from now.

Know you personally, your pain, unearned.
Are you so different from baby burned
With cigarette, every cry spurned?

So, why won't I
Just tell you why?

I owe no answer to any man,
Woman, or child
To change My Plan

Why does it take so many hurt?
I owe no answer.
I AM.
My purpose includes you.

Were you there when I died alone?
I breathed My last, your sin atoned?
I've Lazarus here next to My heart,
A place for you too, when done, your part.

I say who lives. I say who dies.
No one may question or toss Me whys.

It's My way.

Tortured souls are precious.
You will know when you see Me.
You will see the value of your life now
Can't compare to life to be.

I don't answer your question Why.
It's necessary.
And I
AM.

Look Up

God Speaking January 11, 2017

My ways are higher than your ways:
My reasons are My own.
There's nothing too great for God days:
Will I give you an egg or a stone?

Loving isn't a thing I do,
A feeling you like to feel.
Love is Who I AM, but you
Want to know it's real.

I'm real, I'm Truth, won't step aside
While you decry your life.
Did you choose in Me abide?
I led you into strife.

The testing and the breaking are
What makes you like My Son.
He bore your sin, and insofar,
Ransomed every one.

He bled and died unclothed, alone,
Surrounded by the throng.
Was crucified, interred in stone:
Not so much as a song.

Just so you know, you're Mine now.
Your life belongs to Me.
Redeemed from death and so how
You spend your life's not free.

So, who owes who, and what's the catch?
See, worship is the point.
You must forgive, not light the match.
Oil burnt cannot anoint.

Forgiving the Forgiver?
That's possible, but trite.
Rage just makes you quiver;
Passive won't end the fight.

You chose the path unfeeling:
Whatever comes will come.
But all the joy you're stealing
Denies the Light: God's Son.

So, tell Me, would you punish God?
Just how will you do that?
Christ suffered at His Father's nod
While watchers cursed and spat.

If even Christ was never spared
The worst that men can do,
Why expect your life not bared?
It means My hand's on you.

Look up . . . your life is about to change.

Hello, Jesus

Inspired by God May 18, 2010

Hello . . . Jesus?

I've run 'til I can't find my way back again.
I've used and abused any good I had within.
Now I'm empty and alone,
And I'm worthless to my kin.

I was tough! But now I'm broken,
And I've come down to the end.
Prison isn't just a token,
It's a place without a friend.

Where are *You*? Once You loved me,
But I've lived far away from truth.
I don't need someone to judge me, saying,
"What a poor excuse."

What I want is a way out
Of this mess some call a life.
I am tired of the bravado;
I want to rest, to make it right.

When I was young, some old man said
Jesus could wash all my sins away.
But there's no way the mess I'm in
Could ever be made straight one day.

Still, I cannot stop the thoughts that come
Unbidden, unwanted, to my mind.
I barely remember people smiling
In a place left far behind.

Voices

I remember hearing singing
From the church across the road,
And the day that lady gave me
A little Bible for my toad.

I thought she'd scream,
But she just thanked me,
Smiled, and touched my dirty cheek.
And I watched her pull a hankie
Out to wrap up my toad Squeak.

I couldn't read, but hid that Bible
Where my step pa wouldn't see
'Cause he'd have ripped it,
Stomped it, burned it
Just 'cause it belonged to me.

I've still got that little Bible.
The cover's stiff; it's seen its time.
But it's one of very few things
That I can truly say is mine.

And I'm wondering, if I open it,
If I'll find something for my time,
For a man who's out of options,
Who can't be fixed by someone kind.

Can I call you? Can I hear you?
Will you answer if I call?
Will you hear me? I'm a sinner
Got no further I can fall.

But I see I need a savior,
One that understands the drill,
Who's been kicked and beat and spit on,
Who has faced the men who kill.

Even death could not defeat You;
You came back and proved them wrong.
Now I need You to be my champion.
Come and get me, make me strong

On the inside where it's not measured
By my swagger or my lip,
But by what's not seen by others
Without eyes to see my slip.

Please forgive me.
I believe you are God's Son.
I believe God sent you here.
To save this stupid, shipwrecked one.

I believe you died for sinners
Yet were sinless to the end
I believe you rose that morning;
And took your own life back again.

I believe that You can save me.
I believe this Bible's true.
But I come to you with shame.
It's the hardest thing I have to do.

Now I feel something around me.
I can hear and *taste* Your Light.
I've brought nothing I can give You;
And You say, "That's all right."

You accept me and You want me.
Why You do, I'll never know.
But I'll take what You're offering
And I'll never let it go.

I want more. I just want closer.
I must see You. I've got to touch You.
I want to know You. Really know You.

I want this life that You are offering.
I want to live! To feel brand new.
I want to help, I want to love,
I want to show my gratitude.

For I can feel the change inside.
It's like I'm whole, wanted, complete.
I want these others to know you too:
The One who's never known defeat.

Today, You made me a child of God.
In time, I'll resemble You a lot.
Now the darkness has been shattered,
A brand new life is what I've got.

I have called You. I can hear You!
And You *answered* when I called!
Yes, You heard me, just a sinner
With no farther left to fall.

You knew I would need a Savior
Who'd been backed against the wall.
I was lost, but You're my champion
'Cause You have triumphed over *all*!

I finally know You!
You live in my heart.

Hello, Jesus.

How Long, O Lord?

Psalm 13 paraphrased

Inspired by God December 17, 2014

Have You forgotten me, Lord?
Are You hiding Your face from me for a reason?
Do You see my sorrow?
When will You end this dry season?

The darkness sticks to my soul.
Lift me into Your light.
Let me run and laugh again
In the day of joy, sun-bright.

Knowledge is useless in darkness.
How can I see to proceed?
When will the depths of despair
Become like shallows with reeds?

Lighten the eyes of my faith.
Loosen my groping by trust.
I yearn to behold Your face
Long before I am mere dust.

Enemies rejoice when I'm shaken.
The sorrow cleaves day after day.
I turn to you for my solace
As my reddened eyes look your way.

How long, O Lord, must I wait here?
How many prayer words repeat?
Bring your sure mercies to bear now.
Rescue from sunken defeat.

I will remember Your mercy.
I will lift my voice in song.
This will all pass in Your Presence.
You will touch, heal all that's wrong.

You will not leave me here moping.
You've scheduled more good to come.
My task: recounting Your blessings,
Lose sight of self in the Son.

Glory, all glory, is Yours, Lord.
Nothing else matters, is real.
Here I will stand up and worship.
Here will recount former zeal.

Insofar as I am able,
I choose to look up.

The Same

God Speaking October 18, 2014

Your thoughts are not the same
One minute to the next.
Today there in My Word you found
Translations, but same text.

My ways above your ways,
My thoughts above your thoughts,
If your thoughts always change
And few of them are caught,

Trade them in for Mine.
I alone don't change.
Forever I AM with you.
Forever I'm the same.

You change your clothes, you change your hair,
You're always intervening:
Your health, your schedule, and your chair,
New information gleaning.

Who said what to whom and when
Can change your inner world.
You're instant on offensive
When bitter words are hurled.

But I'm the same, I do not change.
I'm not surprised to hear men's lies.
I still forgive so you can live.
I AM your God. I still supply.

I AM . . . the same.

Always I AM faithful with you,
Leading in and out of trial
Meant to bend and break and mold you
Into trusting, holy child

Who becomes the man envisioned
When I saw you long ago.
Or the woman, child, yet leader;
Saw My word within you grow.

You are changed. I AM the same.
You know Me now more than did then.
You trust My Word to safely guide
Through Son Who's God come down to men.

Though all around you changes daily:
Work, friends, food, news, hair, shoes, clothes,
I don't change; I'm still the same,
Can't be compared to any of those.

I AM . . . the same.

The God that Moses knew so well,
The One who spoke creation,
Came in Jesus to redeem
Souls from every nation,

Offers still: Come, buy and eat
Without money, without price
What your soul needs to survive:
Faith, belief, and trust in Christ.

Never has the message changed,
Never lost its urgency.
Come and try Me, come and see.
I give rest and I set free.

I AM. I do not change.
You will find Me when you look:
The God of heaven, Lord of Life;
The story's told within my book.

I . . . AM the same.

You'll find forgiveness, you'll find peace.
There is rest from suffering.
Nothing too hard to overcome
When to the cross you cling.

It's been the same for thousands of years
And still the offer stands:
Come unto Me; I'll give you rest.
It's all part of My plan.

I AM . . . the same

Yesterday . . . today . . . forever.

Set Free Indeed

Alone

Inspired by God October 28, 1996

Empty and alone, the hours stretch before me.
Empty and alone,
Like a house, with empty walls.
My soul feels battered, tired, and worn,
For the battle rages long,
And my strength is gone.

Hopeless thinking makes me vow
No help is on the way,
And in my darkness search for a scrap
Of white cloth to display.

I see a long-forgotten book.
Seems so familiar,
I take a look.

I see names out of my past:
Mark and Titus, Timothy
Unseen, a tear slides down my cheek
For the days when I was free.

Now I'm wondering how my God,
Who promised angels at my feet,
Could allow me to go through *this*

Alone

Then my eye falls on a chapter
And a beam lights up a verse:
I will not leave you nor forsake you
Seems no promise, but a curse.

For I'm left alone in torment
In this place I can't escape.
Then I hear His sweet voice calling
And I know there's no mistake.

Cast all your cares and *I AM with you*
I'm my Beloved's and He is mine
I hear in ripples flowing through me;
Seem like words of nursery rhyme.

The battle is the Lord's
Now I know I'm not alone.
But a sweet peace reaches o'er me
And I know as I am known.

I dream I'm dancing once again
In the dapple 'neath the trees
And I hear my own voice laughing,
Meet my Savior on my knees.

Soon I hear the battle raging,
First far off, then drawing near,
And I'm brought back to the present
Where I'd lived in doubt and fear.

But I find I'm not disheartened
At the enemy's approach.
For his lies and taunts fall brittle
Where before he'd seized my throat.

So, I speak the name of Jesus
With assurance and aplomb,
Now, suddenly, I see I'm winning!
Spirit strong, my mind grows calm.

And I see the battle clearly
Was completely in my mind.
I remember Christ is Victor
Over death and for all time.

Now I take my place in battle
With my armor donned with grace,
And I fight on, "slaying dragons"
Joyous strength fresh from His face.

And know . . .
I never *was* . . .
Alone.

feelings

God Speaking December 28, 2016

Child, you are mine.
I will never leave you or forsake you.
You cannot be lost or separated
From Me in any way.
Ever.

These feelings of abandonment
Are just that: feelings.
You do not want to live by what you feel,
For feelings change many times a day.

Focus on Me. I alone never change.
I AM Light with no shadow of turning.

Put your trust wholly in Me
And let others make their own choices.
You will find that when you stop clinging,
They will stay more often than not.

You be responsible for how you feel.
Own your feelings, and remember:
They are just feelings.

Don't sit and think about how you feel,
Go do something nice for someone else
And the bad feelings will go.

When you help someone
Who cannot do for themselves,
Both of you are blessed.
Get up and go.

Where? Well, tell Me,
Is there a nursing home near you?
Go spread some cheer, fluff a pillow,
Listen to someone who needs to be heard,
And let it roll off of you.

Don't take on another's offense.
In order to remove it,
You will try to pass it on in gossip.

Just be.
Don't take them to raise;
Just listen.

And *smile*! Give away
As many smiles as you can today!
Just do it.

You'll have so much to think about,
You won't have time
To think about yourself.

Have a nice day!

So Alone

Inspired by God December 28, 2016

Father, I come,
Broken, alone.
Don't know how I'll make it
Here on my own.

Too many times,
Rejected outright.
Sick and so tired
Of the constant fight.

Just when I think
I've found a friend,
I say something wrong,
It all comes to an end.

When I feel safe
In new friend I've found,
Reveal who I am,
They don't stick around.

What's wrong with me
That no one can love?
Everyone leaves,
Can't wait to get rid of.

And, why, when they're leaving
Do they say it's me?
Why offer excuses
'Stead go, let be?

I want to be happy
And have a good life
With someone committed,
Husband and wife.

Am I just that awful,
Not fit as a friend,
No man, woman, child
Wants to stay to the end?

What about You, God?
Have You left me too?
I'm really alone here
If I can't trust You.

I'm crying.
Can you hear me?

Never Alone

God Speaking December 28, 2016

You're calling;
I hear you.
I'm closer than breath.
Nothing between us,
Not even death.

Always I'm with you,
For I AM Light.
Today it looks hopeless,
Perception midnight.

Don't build here a dwelling
Of pity alone,
Expecting no better
Than what you've been shown.

Many downtrodden
Need you for a friend:
Someone who's been there.
You're who I'll send.

You be the one
They will find they can trust.
You stay in their life,
No matter the fuss.

You want another
Who'll stay to the end?
You be that person;
You be that friend.

Work hard for others,
Show mercy to them.
Leave fault out of it;
Your pain will end.

Trust as a child
As though never been hurt.
Give love unquestioning,
Steady, not spurt.

When there is trouble,
Don't just run away.
Reach out in love;
Prove that *you'll* stay.

Be first to confess,
Be first to forgive,
Be humble and helpful;
Live and let live.

When you're found trustworthy,
Who can will then stay.
But even if they don't,
With a blessing go away.

You come to Me;
I'm always with you.
Let Me be the constant,
The One Friend who's true.

Live in My Peace
Together, alone.
Keep seeking Me;
I AM your home.

When you do,
You will find
You are *never* . . . alone.

Dying Moments

Inspired by God March 21, 2015

Lord, here I am before You.
Clumsy, I come, solely to You.
Nothing I bring, no offering to make,
No promise enough, nothing I can do.

Here I stand, I kneel, I bow,
Waiting quiet for You to see me.
Nothing I am, I have, or can do
Is enough to make me free.

I come.

The eleventh hour, I come.
Lift me by Your power; I come
In these dying moments of the day.

I come.

Waiting for a sign You've heard,
Waiting for a single word
Giving me a ray of hope
Tomorrow will come,
Your Love break through,
When these dying moments
Bring me to You.

Show me how to let go of the past.
Help me let You see behind my mask.
Shine Your Love inside me; drive out fear.
Bring the Peace that loosens sin through tears.

Here I am, I'm real right now,
Knowing You see me here tonight,
Trusting You to make wrongs right,
Putting here before You all my plight,
Jesus, I come.

In these dying moments
When I bare to You my heart,
Hold me close, whisper forgiveness,
Now let cleansing start.

Help me face myself here,
Be honest as I can,
Admit my sin, release to You,
Right now, begin again.

Help me to let go,
Let You have everything.
Roll it on You who died for me,
My Savior, Lord, and King.

Then walk away free and leave it there,
Remember in days to come
It's not my sin but Yours now,
Each memory, morsel, crumb.

Tonight, I die remembering
In shame my words and deeds.
But in the ashes of my pain,
I see the little seeds

Of new life glowing with Your Light
Now growing bright in me.
And joy comes whelming, bringing tears,
New life is mine—forgiven, free.

And when tomorrow I awaken,
Bring the memory
Not of the pain, but of the gain
With love words: You to me.

And in the days to come I pray
That I will live in You
So when the enemy brings guilt,
I hand that over too.

Delivered from what I cannot change,
I praise You joyously,
Honestly face future in peace:
In Christ, I'm finally free.

Because I see
You with me.

I died to sin, I died to self,
I died to all my past.
I'm born again, I'm new within
And I know at the last
When all my days are used up,
I will see You face to face.
What joy 'twill be when I am free
In my dying moments.

The Past

God Speaking December 31, 2016

Child, I AM with you forever.
I know you; you are Mine.
I AM able to deliver.
I AM mercy; I am kind.

You received My invitation,
Heard the knock at your heart's door.
And you answered, you accepted.
Now, you're Mine forevermore.

I longed for you to know Me
Before you drew first breath.
I knew that you would love Me
And knew, too, you would fret.

Remembering deeds past,
You'd long to erase.
Had to learn the true meaning
Of blood-covering Grace.

I knew you as a sinner;
And I paid for your sin.
I see you as the winner
I now live within.

And My true salvation
Is Love's righteousness.
My death, resurrection
Paid *all*, nothing less.

Walk on in My Glory
I'm before, behind.
In My eyes, sin atoned for;
I'm Master of time.

Don't live in the past,
Don't regret; let it go.
I am back there with you
Yet here and in tomorrow.

And when the day comes
You must answer to God,
I AM your advocate.
Love sees you unflawed.

You live here in time
Where all measure themselves
Against others daily,
Like books lining shelves.

But every, each, only,
Unlikened to any
Whom I have redeemed,
Are perfect already.

So, do not compare
Unless to see Me
In others you meet.
Like you, are they free?

The ones who don't know Me,
You're set here to tell.
They know they are sinners.
Speak of hope in you dwells.

I AM Blessed Hope
Redeeming mankind

From curse found in judgment;
Died once for all time.

Holy crucifixion,
The way of the cross,
Paid once for all sin:
Purposed none would be lost.

But the liar called Satan
Would have men believe
There's no hope, so why bother?
"Sin better! Serve me!"

So, they keep comparing,
To see who's the worst.
Egged on by deceiver,
Live under the curse.

Tell them I love them.
If only one hears,
That's one more for Glory,
Repenting in tears.

My offer, accepted,
Puts new smile on face.
Burdens roll onto Me:
Another thankful for grace.

Don't live in the past;
It won't change a thing.
Move forward in Grace;
Speak oft of your King . . . of kings.

Close

Inspired by God December 29, 2016

Close but not completed,
Close but no cigar.
I tried to do everything right;
Close but still so far.

Intentions, plans and prophecies
All pointed to the way.
Minute decisions turned the course
To where I am today.

It should have been,
I might have done,
It started right,
Could have been won.

I took a turn,
To take a look,
Could not go back,
An hour it took.

An hour that changed
My course forever.
How could I know
The ties I'd sever?

Now I see
What might have been,
Where I am now,
Where I was then.

Why can't I keep
Your Word I know?
What I should do,
Where not to go.

But I don't do it.

What answer
Will I give You

When I come?

Difficult Times

A Word from the Lord

God Speaking December 1, 2014

Daughter One, you are ashamed
Of your behavior in a part of your life.
I see the good in you during that same time.

You see the sin and compromise
And fool that you were.
I see the child of God I call Mine
Who was learning of Me,
Worshipping Me,
Serving Me.

You see how you were manipulated.
I see how you submitted to Me
And let Me use you for good.
You see your poor choices.
I see your faithfulness.

You made one of the hardest choices
Of your life during that time
And you saw it through
Because it was the right thing to do
And it honored My Word.

You walked through a difficult depression
And still served faithfully at church.
And I have written in My book
The haunting prayers you prayed
To stay away from sin.

I was with you
When you had to make the choice
All over again
To do the right thing.

I was with you
When you said the wrong thing years later,
Plunging you back into
The same wrong relationship.

I saw you voluntarily give up
Being right many times in mercy.
You fulfilled your vow
And repeatedly asked My forgiveness
For your sin.

You gave your life for a friend.
I wrote it down.
No one in heaven judged you.
Not one.

Not . . . One.

You grieve your love.
In heaven, it is valued by all.
You see it as a moral failure.
In heaven, your constancy
Is seen as a victory.

Your battle with self
And right and wrong
And values
Was a spiritual struggle.

And there were many battles
In the heavenlies
As you prayed
Silently or out loud.

And in the end,
The soul you asked Me to save
Became Mine.

No greater love has any man than this:
That he lay down his life for his friend.

Wipe the tears,
Lift the head,
And worship.

I AM with you.

Come

God Speaking December 29, 2016

Child, you're Mine,
Have always been.
I've heard you laugh
And watched you grin.

With every breath,
I've been with you.
The good, the bad,
The hard times too.

When you took off
The wrong way,
You felt conviction,
Knew you'd pay.

You'd given your word,
You'd not go back.
You kept your promise,
Though conscience wracked.

You stayed that course
Long as you could,
Then turned to Me.
I knew you would.

I cleansed, you cried,
You'd made a mess.
I used for good,
But what a test.

You'd always hoped
You'd get it right.
Willing to stand,
And even fight.

You think your life
Would sure have stayed
Much better if
You'd just obeyed.

No, it wouldn't.

You see, each trial's
What made you strong.
You only saw
That you were wrong.

"If only" still
Haunts you today.
I view you different,
Better way.

Know Paul had shipwrecks,
You wrecked too.
John faced starvation,
You fought the blues.

Men wrote the gospel,
My story stands.
And now I've placed it
In your hands.

You've faced your test
And still you live.
Encouraging,
Fresh hope you give.

To others tossed,
Think they're no good,
Tell them your tale:
With Me you stood.

Are standing still
And pressing on.
When you see Me,
T'will be all gone.

And you'll be clothed
In My righteousness.

It's not how you get here,
It's that you come.

No Matter

God Speaking April 2015

No speck or mote or beam or rod
Shall ever mar your eye
For longer than it takes to shout,
"Oh, Lord, remove! Please take it out!
Open my eyes that I may see
The truth You would reveal to me."

No matter
No matter

There's nothing that can come between.
You're in My hand, My Glory seen
On you as you trust in each hour
Things you can't keep, world would devour.
For all that's yours is loosely held,
Your eye on Me, My Spirit welled.

No matter
No matter

The trials this life is cluttered by
Bring anger, tears into your eye,
I use to shape your holy state,
I use to change you, are your fate.
For when in time the hard part's done,
You'll look like Me, the victory won.
And say

No matter
No matter

When you and I stand face to face
Right here in Glory, Heaven-place,
You'll look like Me, complete and whole,
And with the throng, each ransomed soul,
Shout "Glory!"
You'll see . . .

No matter
No matter what
No matter

The Last Prisoner

Inspired by God September 20, 2014

Lord, I already forgave.
I let it go, I blessed,
And I was released.

It took time; it took work.
I had to do it again.
And again . . .
And again.

But I still hurt sometimes.
I still regret.
I can't undo
Any of it.

Now I see I forgave,
But I didn't count
Everyone slain
By the pain.

I didn't forgive . . . me.

No matter how I see it,
Any angle I choose,
It always comes out
The same:

The pain
Still stabs
And stabs
And stabs.

I can't stop punishing myself.
I am a prisoner still.

Lord, You will have to do it.
It's too hard.
It's too deep.
It's too real.
It's too painful.
I can't do it alone.
I can't do it on my own.

So, I open my scarred,
Still-broken heart.
It limps and gimps
And yet goes on.

I open myself to You.
Completely open . . .
To You.

Lying on the table
For the Surgeon.
Laid out on the altar,
Willing sacrifice.

Take this life,
This painful life,
And I will trust
In You.
You alone.

Completely alone . . . with me.
I am . . .the last prisoner.

Love My Neighbor, My Enemy

Inspired by God December 6, 2015

Love my neighbor
As myself.
Which neighbor?

The one I can see
The one that I meet
The one in my house
The one I don't know
The one with a need

The invisible one
The loud one
The abusive one
The parent
Or child
Or orphan
Or ugly one

The least of these
Is my neighbor.

How *do* I love?
I open and offer myself
I listen and wait
And God shows me
He died to redeem
My neighbor.

Love my enemy.
I ask You to open my eyes.
Who is my enemy?

The one I can see
Who doesn't like me,
Maybe hates me
Or hates people like me.

The one who has reason to hate
Has reason to kill
You said love my enemy.

How do I do that?
I can't,
But You can.
Lord, love through me.

Do good through me
To those who hate me,
Those who despitefully use me.

I listen and wait
And You show me
You died to redeem
My enemy.

David asked You
To fight his battles,
Subdue his enemies,
Wipe 'em out.

Jesus said
Love 'em.

Love my enemy
Who lives in my house,
The one who finds fault,
Argues, belittles.
The one who's unhappy
And wishes me gone.

How can I love
When those things
Stand between us?

Who *is* my enemy?

What if it's *me*?

Keep Walking

God Speaking September 28, 2015

I AM for you always.
Favor now is yours.
Sin has been the problem.
My blood is the cure.

Now your motivation is
The Love you have inside.
Now you long to please Me,
My love you cannot hide.

Forty-'leven promises
"If you, then I," they say.
You've found you're living better with
Those promises each day.

Joy inside is simmering;
With peace you face all comers.
You better understand Me
And fewer thoughts are bummers.

There is new revelation
Every time you search My Word.
My still, small voice your guide now,
You follow what you've heard.

When one in you confided,
You heard, "Tell her your story."
She later said you'd told her life;
She gave Me all the Glory.

My Peace stays with her since that day
She laid her burden down.
She walks in hope; she's stronger now.
I have her victor's crown.

You are My hands and feet on earth
To share the words I said.
Encourage with your prayers and words
And deeds. Stand in My stead.

Keep running for the prize until
The day I bring you home.
Guard your heart and keep your eyes
On Me, so they won't roam.

And all the hard times you face now
Will then seem very small.
When you see Me, I welcome,
You'll be glad you gave your all.

You have My strength to see you through,
My joy in who you are,
To climb the path I've given;
Now it's short, not very far.

And soon, you'll be with Me.
You'll feel Me hold you in My arms.
And all you've pictured will be real
With Me, where nothing harms.

I AM with you always
Here in life and on through death.
I've given you each heartbeat,
Gifted you with every breath.

And better gifts are waiting;
From My storehouse, I provide.
Walk on in faith; live in My Word.
Let it in you reside.

I AM with you on this journey
And I'll bring you safe to Me.
You will see Me as I AM,
As King of kings, of Holy Three

Who are One.

It's done.
Keep walking.

Chosen to Serve Me

The Police Officer

Inspired by God June 30, 2017

Donuts and coffee? Really?
You think I'm your night watchman?
Hey, I went to school for this.
Law and order's not a job; it's a calling.

The hours are long. Paperwork's not done,
Some perp will walk if I don't get it right.
Miranda them up, bring them in, get the facts.
I see already it'll be a long night.

Today I've got a job to do:
Catching speeders, ye gods.
Do it right, I go home.
That means I beat the odds.

Some days are darker:
There are bodies involved,
Traffic inconvenienced,
Crimes to be solved.

Everyone wants justice.
My job: defend.
Some live on their own terms
And others' lives end.

Our new ones get bank jobs,
I'm not talking crime.
Just sit there: a presence,
Putting in time.

It's dues. We all pay 'em.
Tough ones involve blood,
Discharging a weapon
In duty for good.

Knock on a door,
Bring bereavement to kin,
Must have permission
To even step in.

It works on your mind;
Your heart can grow cold.
Drink could be a problem
Before very old.

Anger builds up,
We must visit the shrink;
Go back to duty
With thoughts we still think.

You want us jolly
When we're off the job
And all the time we're aware
We're not God.

So many times, though,
We must react,
Quickly averting
A criminal attack.

We'll never ask you
To lift us in prayer
But we prob'ly need it the most,
If you care.

The demons are many
We fight every day,
Must always be ready
To jump the right way.

Split-second decision
We'll have to defend
Can mean a saved child
Or some life may end.

We're on your streets,
Keeping you safe,
Doing our level best,
Good choices make.

What you can do is appreciate.
Don't sing us a song;
Don't bake us a cake.
(well, maybe)

Respect goes beyond
The core of who we are.
Address us as "officer"
And a smile can go far.

We're doing our duty
All day or each night.
If you're life's complacent,
Then we did it right.

I am a peace officer
Making your day
Better.

My Cop

God Speaking March 28, 2017

Son, if you only knew Who I really AM,
You'd know My Love is not some sham,
You'd know My Peace there deep inside,
You'd know you never have to hide.

I know it all, the things you've done.
I'm well aware when daylight comes,
You're sleeping off the night's hard hours,
The things you've seen: life's broken flowers.

You've worked the nights when children died,
Domestic fights, seen cases tried,
Dodged hard words shouted, bullets fired.
Police work's hard and you get tired.

It has its good side, when things go right.
But that won't happen every night.
Sometimes you glimpse My hand unseen,
Lost child found safe, avoid crime scene.

Sometimes the school zone thing seems boring,
Need no adrenaline, there's no exploring,
Prefer the rush that comes with crime,
Suburban city cop, not the big time.

This, the life I've called you to,
I can call you out of;
You know that's true.

But what you don't know is My Love. Me.
You're worth the waiting 'til you can see.
Why not today? Don't change a thing.
I'll meet you here, salvation bring.

Just think about it.
I'll be here.
I'm always here.

The Firefighter

Inspired by God June 30, 2017

I have been there: massive conflagration
In Scott Airpack, heavy boots, and gloves.
Fought that hose, its hookup, water started,
Saving people losing things they love.

All the training, all the time and effort
Show their worth when families walk away.
Tomorrow's looking good to those we've rescued.
In this job, it's never just another day.

We all are haunted by the ones too soon gone,
Know we can't save them all, but we sure try.
We lock it down, go on to save the next ones.
Today's tired, sweaty success: no one died.

The work is hard and heavy; it takes muscle.
When action starts, need rush to get 'er done.
We work safe, have backs of brother firemen,
Want everyone go home, daughter or son.

The big ones are the times a forest catches,
We scramble, parachute into the fray.
It takes us all to get the beast to buckle.
We work that bitch hard day and night and day.

I'll be honest, I love what I'm doing.
Adrenaline kicks in, I'll whip the world.
I've learned the tricks of wind and time and lightning,
Been one of many where the flames have swirled.

You want to help? Keep us on your prayer list.
Ask the Lord be with us, keep us safe,
Bring us home to our kids, spouses, families,
Give us one more day to come awake.

We need your support, know you respect us.
We have our own motives doing this for you.
Just let us know you notice . . . oops, I hear it!
Gotta go! The claxon's blaring through!

My Firemen

God Speaking August 17, 2017

You may have loved it all your life
Or come to it farther along.
Sooner or later though, fire would draw you,
The power of it mighty and strong.

You have a life path that swung by this way;
Safety's now more than a word.
Training learned here has built muscle, respect.
Confident, ply what you've heard.

You're always ready, stand willing to serve.
Part of a team, you connect.
Much more than hoses, or buddy the axe,
The men who serve as you direct.

You take your job seriously every new day,
Stay up on the latest equipment.
Make every training, attend yearly fire school;
You even take new firetruck shipment.

The best thing you do is respect fellow firefighters,
No matter if woman or man.
You're in it together and answer the call.
Every time, I hold all in My hand.

I'm with you each time you serve, ride the truck.
I'm there in your small airpack world.
My angels oft cover you when you get stuck
And guide you to scared, lost child curled.

I could even tell you just how many times
A timber burned through, didn't fall.
And it is My Spirit in you that just knows
A flashover's coming; don't stall.

There's nothing so difficult to face in this job
As the service for one who has fallen.
And never a prouder moment for truck
Than to carry that firefighter's coffin.

I'm proud of My firemen, though all are full grown.
I help you do your job and well.
I want to remind you you're never alone.
I'm with you. I wanted to tell . . .

All of you . . .

I'm proud of My firemen.

The Soldier

Inspired by God July 14, 2017

I will not listen, for you do not know
All I have gone through to get here.
I have fought enemies inside and out
And I am the master of fear.

Nothing can touch me or hurt me or crowd.
I stand alone; I am keen.
Sharpened by battle and honed to cheat death,
I am a killing machine.

I have seen more in my time in the field
Than some other soldiers can bear.
I step right over the shrapnel of bodies:
Enemies no doc can repair.

And still they keep coming.
They're fierce and they're mean.
Well, I'm meaner still, and I see
They'll stop at nothing and I will keep fighting,
Stay low so no bullet finds me.

I can't afford to consider my family,
To let my mind wander at all.
For that could be moment
My buddy needs cover.
In war, every back's 'gainst the wall.

I've been on furlough; my mind was back there,
Deep in the battle, aware.
There is no rest that can keep my attention.
It's still in my head and I'm there.

I've seen the docs and I've talked to shrinks;
I tell them what they want to hear.
But nothing can reach into what's in my mind.
It's locked down, with no chink for fear.

I'm going back just as soon as they'll let me.
Third tour was worse than the rest.
This next one I'm counting on killing the bad ones.
Yeah, I've got some lead to invest.

I don't have time for this stupid religion crap;
Go sing your syrupy songs.
My mind is focused on doing my job;
The battlefield's where I belong.

Don't think for a moment that I don't know God;
He's with me wherever I go.
I stand here today because He isn't through.
There's much more to do; that I know.

Thanks for your prayers
And the boxes at Christmas.
A letter is more welcome still.

I am a soldier;
I'm trained to bring death,
So, pardon me while I go kill.

The Uniform

God Speaking June 30, 2017

To every man in military uniform, I salute you.
You live the will of God in serving others.
I certainly see you, I AM with you,
And appreciate all you give, all you do
For good, for God, for country.

Whether for a season or as your career,
You carry on your shoulders
The safety of fellow countrymen
Of every gender, race, and creed.

You are conscious of your responsibility
And carry out your orders,
Respecting the flag under which you serve.

Know here and now, I AM with you
No matter which uniform you wear,
Which branch of the armed services insignia
Is on your chest, what rank or gender is yours.

Not only am I with you, I hear your prayers,
I know your thoughts, I see your heart,
And I accept you fully as who you are.

No special words are needed,
For I hear the cry of the heart
In that one shouted word: GOD!!!

You will do what duty demands
Just as My Son did.

You will complete
Every assignment
With integrity
Because you fully respect
Your commanding officers.

If they are not worthy of your respect,
I request that you obey them instead
With the respect that is due to Me,
For I have given them authority over you
For My purpose.
By obeying them, you obey Me.

I honor you for your service to men
Performed as unto the Lord.

Amen.

My Servants
God Speaking July 14, 2017

Called out of darkness and into My Light,
Each of you came the hard way.
I've honed you to strengthen
Through tough circumstance,
By Grace stand before Me this day.

You've My respect.
You are strong and you stand,
Take nothing off *any*one.
I've called you here and I have made sure
You know Who I AM: Holy One.

You talk to Me; you believe that I AM.
You're often aware I am near,
Acknowledge respectfully each, every time
You come through a close one still here.

Do you know My Son? If you open your heart
And you ask Him, He will come in.
He already knows all the worst things about you;
It's His blood that covers your sin.

I want you with Me.
When you die, you will come.
You will stand before His judgment throne.

There'll be just one question
You'll want to get right:
Does He know you?
By Him are you known?

Everything else is covered by Grace,
Even the words you have spoken.
But it is your heart that determines your fate.
Is Jesus in there?
If He is,
Then your heart once was broken.

Author

About the Author

Hi, I'm Karen J Chisholm, a pianist, singer, songwriter, poet, author living in Houston, Texas.

Voices is the third book of Poems Inspired by God, preceded by I AM with You, and Tough as Nails. I love writing for Father, being His scribe, learning his view of what we go through, hearing his encouragement, knowing His Grace is unlimited and He is for us. Always.

He said His vision for the first book, I AM with You, is to put it in hands around the world. I am praying for just that, and am thankful for the opportunity to serve Him.

You can visit my webpage www.karenjchisholm.com to hear some of the songs God has given me and read some of the poems He has let me scribe for him.

On the website, there is a tab with blogs I have shared. What He says always seems so precious, and it makes me really think about the deep things of God that infuse our daily life. His steadfast Love keeps me going. He never judges. He only encourages, and I love working for Him.

I am Music Director at my church and we sing the songs He gives me there along with hymns and choruses. When I am not writing for God or putting the songs He gives me into shareable format, I enjoy my family.

Sometimes I lead worship at retreats or speak for groups, conferences, monthly meetings, or even one-on-one, sharing God's words and songs of encouragement, blessing, and the Presence of God.

I would be interested in hearing how the poems in this book touched your life, encouraged you, or 'read your mail.' And, if you send me a prayer request, I will gladly pray for you. karen@karenjchisholm.com

God bless you!

www.ingramcontent.com/pod-product-compliance
Lightning Source LLC
Chambersburg PA
CBHW020911090426
42736CB00008B/577